6/00

With a Moon in Transit

ALSO BY JACQUELINE OSHEROW

Looking for Angels in New York
Conversations with Survivors

With a Moon in Transit

JACQUELINE OSHEROW

Grove Press
New York

Published simultaneously in Canada
Printed in the United States of America

FIRST EDITION

Library of Congress Cataloging-in-Publication Data

Osherow, Jacqueline.
    With a moon in transit / Jacqueline Osherow. — 1st ed.
        p.   cm.
    ISBN 0-8021-1599-3
    I. Title.
PS3565.S545W58   1996
811'.54 — dc20   96–18201

Grove Press
841 Broadway
New York, NY 10003

10 9 8 7 6 5 4 3 2 1

For Saul, Magda, Dora and Mollie

Acknowledgments

Antioch Review: "Early Spring, Back in London"

The New Republic: "Somebody Ought to Write a Poem for Ptolemy," "Breezeway, circa 1964," "Beijing Rids Itself of Sparrows"

The Paris Review: "Brief Encounter with a Hero, Name Unknown," "On a City I Meant to Visit, Now at War," "My Cousin Abe, Paul Antschel and Paul Celan"

Partisan Review: "Calling Emily Dickinson to Come, as Guide, Out West"

Pivot: "Calm Day at Couminole" and "Villanelle for the Middle of the Night"

Ploughshares: "Terza Rima for a Sudden Change in Seasons"

Prairie Schooner: "On My Third Daughter's First Night Home"

Quarterly West: "Sonnet about Last Night's Moon beneath the Clouds"

Radcliffe Quarterly: "Two Sonnets for the Wind in the Leaves"

Southwest Review: "London, Before and After: the Middle Way"

Triquarterly: "Moses in Paradise"

Western Humanities Review and *The Best American Poetry, 1995*: "Late Night Tête-à-tête with a Moon in Transit"

The author gratefully acknowledges the assistance of the MacDowell Colony and the Utah Arts Council in writing this book. She is also extremely grateful to George Bradley, Wayne Koestenbaum and Barry Weller for their invaluable support.

Contents

V

I

Late Night Tête-à-tête with a Moon in Transit

Che fai tu, luna, in ciel, dimmi, che fai,
Silenziosa luna?

I've always wished I could have asked that question,
Though I'm not one to ask that sort of thing
And I'd probably spoil it in translation;

Besides, the moon won't tell me what it's doing,
Caught, like a wayward kite, up in that tree,
And reaching for a cloud's extended wing . . .

But I'd still love to float some words above me
To palm stray silver or maybe panhandle
The leaves' new-minted coins from that flush tree.

Usually I write these things to people,
But why not, since no one else is listening,
Address myself to you, *luna in ciel,*

Who have left the tree, the cloud, are no doubt hastening
To strain the face of some unknowing city
With your own relentless questioning.

Do you remember that time in Newark, when you took pity
On the semi-burnt-out towers at the city's rim?
Maybe it was just a show of vanity,

That you make things of beauty even of them
And their misshapen friends, the cast-iron bridge
And pockmarked stretch of road that hauled me home:

Sudden adornments on an orange, huge,
Dome-shaped temple rising from the ground
To which a desperate skyline had made pilgrimage,

Its high-rises prostrate on the holy ground,
Like throngs in Mecca, hearing their muezzin.
And there was Newark, momentarily crowned—

As if by that ecstatic, praying din—
For once in its stunted life with gold, not thorns,
A colossal halo where its sky had been,

Seeming to say that when a city burns
It doesn't actually have to be consumed.
I suppose, if there's a God, these are His concerns,

But you'd know better than I; it's you He named,
On the fourth day, by name, and there you were.
You still arrive as if you'd just been dreamed

Out of nothing by a reckless dreamer's dreamer,
Or, rather, out of nothing but a word.
Did you hear it called or was it all a blur—

The stars' wild glittering, a fish, a bird,
Howling animals, a man, a woman
And, before you'd settled in, their young son murdered . . .

I wonder if you caught a glimpse of sun
Before you had to go your separate ways.
Perhaps, in all this time, you've never known

About the routine epochs we call days
When a good deal less of what we are is hidden.
You're off wandering in a foreign maze

Of branches, wires and rooftops, until a sudden
Undoing of the darkness sends you back to us.
But I've seen you, in the daytime, come unbidden,

As if you preferred to be anonymous,
A tiny, unassuming, moon-shaped cloud
Half trying to hide, half to spy on us.

Perhaps that's what you were doing in Leningrad
When I took a walk at dusk along the Nevsky Prospekt
And caught you setting up a masquerade

As one of the heavy globes that intersect
The once grand boulevard at every step,
Lighting the way for palaces, absurdly decked—

Like stout, old matrons in a bridal shop—
In frilly and unflattering pastels.
You hovered over them as if to eavesdrop

As they murmured to their doubles in canals,
Your deadpan face unnaturally low
And white light clinging to their scarred pastels

Until they seemed to fill with early snow.
You were still there when I entered my hotel
But you must've risen eventually; you had to

Once you'd heard what they were willing to tell.
Maybe they recited a local poem
In which the Neva casts her murky spell,

A great one, maybe, like the Requiem
Extorted from the woman in gray-blue shards of paint
Who presides over the Russian Art Museum

Along with several icons of a Russian saint—
Nicholas, maybe?—and a lone Chagall.
She—though I'd never read her—managed to haunt

My travels just by staring from that wall.
Now I'd scour the city for some mirage
Of her, in the House on the Fontanka, at her table

Coaxing warring ghosts onto a page
From their flimsy strongholds in the air.
In those days, all I cared for was the Hermitage:

Simone Martini's Mary, bent to hear,
But cut away from her announcing angel,
Deep blue robes engulfing all of her

(Their color, egg whites crushed with lapis lazuli)
To frame each long white hand's elaborate wing
And the features streaming down her twisted, frail

Face intent, exquisitely, on nothing.
I saw her counterpart in Washington years later:
An all-gold angel, tiny, glittering,

Also Simone Martini's, also pure,
Olive branch in hand, hailing the wall,
His message reaching to the North Atlantic somewhere

To be salvaged by a pious, passing seagull
Who flew to Leningrad, as if on pilgrimage,
And circled the museum screaming *Hail*

Unless he was trying, moon, to pay *you* homage—
With his faith he could see you in the daytime
Despite your elaborate camouflage—

Or maybe to the huge Matisses in the museum,
So bright they grabbed his keen eye through the windows.
Is that what *you* were doing, moon? Staring at them:

The lavish dining room, the couple in pajamas,
Palm fronds on Morocco's stucco domes,
And next to a squatting outdoor orchestra's

Scraggly band, with knees and hands for drums:
That iron-pumping remake of *La Danse*,
Inspired, doubtless, by the high, taut limbs

Of the Ballets Russes' still unmatched Nijinsky
Who'd stay limber for an endless quarter century
At the window of his dull asylum in France,

Listening for the wind to stir a tree
With a long legato like the solo moan
That slithered down, then up, the flute that Debussy

Commissioned to awake his sleeping faun.
Who knows what Anastasia would wait
For at the window of *her* asylum — French? Italian?

She remembered nothing, not the heavy velvet
Her mother made her wear that so encumbered
Her entrance to the royal box, in state,

Where her father, when it darkened, always slumbered
As her mother shed her jewels and ermine cape.
If Anastasia had heard that flute, she'd have remembered

Nijinsky's stunning Grand Finale leap,
Anything besides the string of closed, dark spaces
That constituted her pyrrhic escape.

7

I wonder if she ever saw those huge Matisses,
If Nijinsky saw his likeness in *The Dance*,
If they would even have known each other's faces

If they'd been in the same asylum, in France.
Perhaps they were, already, too much changed—
It wouldn't really have been a great coincidence,

A place known to Russians, who arranged
With a jewel or two, the care for noble émigrés—
Only Matisse's painting is still unchanged:

The exploding torsos, limbs, necks, fingers, toes.
I just saw it hanging in New York,
At least as graceful as it ever was.

That's right, if unbelievable: New York.
Along with all its cronies (well, not all;
They decided—though its picture's in the book—

That *La Musique* was too infirm to travel).
But the people in pajamas, the green Moroccan,
That dining room with roses on its wall,

Were there with several prostrate, white-robed men,
Each of whom resembled a praying dome.
And I'd thought I'd never see those paintings again,

Had sacrificed all Leningrad to see them,
Staying from nine in the morning until dark
Or dusk, rather, in each resplendent room.

But there they all were, hanging in New York.
You were there, too, posing as a water tank
Atop one of the towers that line the park

And then as a new ornament for Citibank.
You'll forgive me, won't you, if I wasn't fooled?
I *was* glad to see you there, absurdist, blank,

Holding your milky own against the cold.
Why should Matisse be more footloose than you?
And why should I have felt so ridiculed

That what I'd made a pilgrimage to know
Had come, of its accord, a dozen years later?
How could anyone have guessed that now

Leningrad would again be named for Peter?
Not the saint so much as the young czar,
Who, posing as a sailor on a freighter,

Found one thing in all the world to long for:
A cluster of islands in a slim lagoon—
Have you ever been there? I've not seen you there,

Though I can't say I was looking for you, moon—
That had spent so long refining their reflection,
Trying first these towers, then these arches, on,

This jagged bridge, this square, this predilection
For a line of marble porticoes, a dome,
That Peter, almost instantly, began construction

Of a copycat version, nearer home,
Where the Neva's ice would copy it again . . .
How his architects must have longed for Rome

Or wherever they'd come from, Florence, Naples, Milan,
Lured by who knows how much Russian gold
And the wild ambition—madness?—of the plan

To clear some empty marshlands near a sea and build,
Of all things, a northern rival to Venice.
The first foundations shattered in the cold

Or floundered in the swamp and mud and ice;
Thousands upon thousands of workers died.
Of what? Drowning? Frostbite? Typhus? Tetanus?

I looked it up, in the encyclopedia, under Leningrad,
And found out Peter never made it to Venice.
He was on his way, but stopped, the entry said,

Because of a rebellion—at home? in Venice?
Who was it who rebelled? Could they have won?
And what had Peter seen that could entice

Such single-minded purpose from a person?
(A Canaletto? An engraving? Was it just the legend?)
Maybe he saw his city in a vision;

It didn't resemble Venice in the end.
Not, of course, that any city could,
Though it is, in its clunky way, certainly grand.

But why am I telling you? You've surely made
An occasional impression on the Grand Canal
Or slipped it silver from behind a cloud

Where you'd set up your temporary arsenal.
But Venice has no need for your loose change
Or for your services as would-be sentinel.

It's one place your white light can't unhinge
Though you might put a word in with the tide
To slow each palace's unconscious plunge

Into the Adriatic's murky bed. . . .
Imagine those canals reflecting only clouds
Like mirrors in a house of mourning, covered.

I ought to have learned by now that each thing fades,
Almost all of them without a trace.
Why should a spot like Venice beat the odds

When we haven't got one relic from Atlantis?
You could probably describe the place in detail,
The pools where you'd admire your still-young face,

The pillars you'd turn nearly blue, the wall
Where a sculpted hero mourned the child-apprentice
Who took himself too near the sun and fell

Into the waiting sea, just like Atlantis
And, soon, now, Venice and the other city-myths
Whose names alone could at one time entice

A thousand dreaming princes to their deaths
As they surveyed building sites for ideal plans,
Scoured continents for masons, sculptors, goldsmiths,

Glaziers, painters, marble, tiny stones
To fill ten thousand ceilings with mosaics,
Not a glint of one of which remains.

But I forget that you're also made of rocks,
Not a wanderer, after all, but a place,
Devoid of even the crudest human tricks.

And your enchantress's serene, pearl face
Is actually nothing more than a reflection.
So whom am I talking to? And what does this

Make me, but a reflection of a reflection,
These lines a sort of verbal hall of mirrors,
Paling copies of copies in each direction

Of the copied plans of czars, doges, emperors,
Not one of them accurate or thorough,
But variants on whimsies, envies, errors,

Something like my long obsession with you;
I, too, would love to alter every city
With my own flawless arsenal of silver-blue

And ignore the pressing accidents of gravity,
Or at least seem to, as you've always done,
And burn whatever's dreary, banal, petty

With a subtle glitter borrowed from a sun
No one on their piece of earth can see.
I'd have a worthwhile answer to your question

If, by some fluke, you should one day call to me—
What's up, loquacious person, what are you doing?—
As you rest against a local cloud or tree,

My face transfixed and overflowing
With so much white and silver that the jealous stars
Would leave their constellations and come following—

The sky a mess of limbless lions and bears,
Stranded centaurs, hunters, wingless swans—
Until they'd rearranged themselves as dancers,

Deposed Russian princesses, lost fauns,
Rebels, painters, architects, pretenders
To a restless century's discarded thrones,

All of them waiting, breathless, at their windows
For even the most diminished kinds of signs,
Except for those few enterprising wanderers

Who scavenge local shores for telltale stones
And could be said, in all their travels, to mimic you.
Perhaps, among them, there are some lucky ones

Who find some rocks from which they can construe
A wall or tower or bridge or an entire town
And then there are those who simply wait for you

To come to them and tell them what you've seen.
I know for a fact you've obliged some of them;
With Akhmatova you had a nightly conversation

And with Peter, disappointed, on his voyage home.
He was lucky, really, not to have seen San Marco;
This way, he was satisfied with one gold dome

And a brick palace covered in yellow stucco.
Perhaps it was you who suggested it,
You who sent Matisse off to Morocco—

So Petersburg is lovely only by your light
And, as a symbol on a mosque, at least,
Matisse was finally forced to paint your portrait.

Poor old moon, I suppose you couldn't resist;
You, too, have suffered great indignities—
Men trampling on you, shuttles roaring past,

Bits of you in all our major cities,
The nighttime sky clogged with manmade rivals—
You, whose likenesses had once been deities,

With sacrifices nightly, temples, festivals.
Now, some nights, you make your rounds as modestly
As a retired civil servant on her travels.

But, still, couldn't you tell me what you see?
I've waited so long, and fairly patiently
Che fai tu, luna, in ciel? Dimmi.

II

Brief Encounter with a Hero, Name Unknown

It could have been a matter of modesty
It could have been the gold sewn in your dress
You might even have feared for your chastity
Maybe it was simple recklessness

Perhaps you couldn't part with that one dress
Once rumpled by a skillful, knowing beau
Or were wearing it to hide a gaping abscess
Or were pregnant and ashamed to let it show

Maybe you'd seen a Western dubbed in Polish
Or Yiddish or Czech or whatever it was you spoke
And remembered some hokey John Wayne flourish
That downed four outlaws at a single stroke

Maybe you were an unexceptional girl
Who'd gone crazy on the claustrophobic ride
Maybe you had had a lovers' quarrel
And, for days, been contemplating suicide

You could have been a fighter in the woods
And drilled this tactic over and over and over
Who knows? Perhaps you thought you'd beat the odds
Maybe it wasn't even the right maneuver

My father-in-law mentioned it in passing
When I asked how well he'd known his SS boss
(His job in Birkenau had been delousing;
They also used the Zyklon B for lice)

And he named one Schillinger, SS
And told how he had watched Schillinger die
When a new woman, ordered to undress
(You were going to the gas chamber, apparently)

Instead grabbed hold of Schillinger's own gun
And killed three other guards along with him
Such things, says my father-in-law, were common
(Needless to say, in seconds you had joined them)

It could have been a matter of modesty
It could have been the gold sewn in your dress
You might even have feared for your chastity
Maybe it was simple recklessness

My Cousin Abe, Paul Antschel
and Paul Celan

O one, o none, o no one, o you
Where did the way lead when it led nowhere?

Perhaps, like everything, it has its flow and ebb,
The way nowhere, I mean, your brutal question.
Not that you were asking me. You asked no one
But I once eavesdropped on the conversation.
Regards, by the way, from my cousin, Abe;
I'm hoping they will serve as introduction.

Do you remember him? For twelve years your classmate?
A Yiddish speaker, religious, quick at math?
I was telling about his great *lantzman*-poet
And he identified you by your death:
He killed himself? In Paris? In the Seine?
His name is Antschel, Paul Antschel, not Celan.

He even has a picture of your graduation
(You were both dark-haired dreamy-eyed young men).
It's a wonder the photograph survived.
My cousin must have brought it to Japan,
A surprising place to go, once the war began,
But, for a while, his uncle's business thrived,

Import-export, I think it was, coral, pearls.
My mother has a strand of heavy beads
That Abe's wife, Beka, brought to her years later,
Like setting suns erased by wisps of clouds.
Abe must have meant them for his mother or sister
Or perhaps even the shiest of the girls

In matching fur-trimmed muffs and collars and hems
Whom you'd watch dawdling on their way to *shul*
While you were working on your weekly themes.
Abe said no one else could win the prize,
That everything you wrote was something beautiful
And he's a hard man, of little praise.

When I asked him more questions, he grew fierce:
Nice? Sure. We were all nice. Nice. Quiet.
Yes. I saw him daily for twelve years
But what do you ever know about a person?
I would speak in Yiddish, he spoke German;
My family was religious, his was not.

He pointed out some others in the picture:
The one who got to Venezuela to manufacture
Was it textiles? The one who managed to hide,
The one who teaches chemistry in Austria;
He didn't bother to say the rest had died
With his mother, his sister, your parents, in Transnistria . . .

As a child, I never dreamed it was a place,
It seemed to me some sort of fatal curse,
The heaviest among the floating words
I'd always heard but couldn't precisely trace.
Transnistria, it was only uttered in whispers
That lingered, unresolved, like bungled chords.

I later learned that Beka's mother had died
In Transnistria, my grandma's brother's wife.
They'd written back and forth, a charming girl,
So gracefully she'd filled sheaf after sheaf:
How they went out picking berries, mushrooms, sorrel . . .
Perhaps she met your parents on the ride.

How she must've made my grandma long for home
When she described her soups of sorrel and mushrooms,
The brandy she would coax from new, ripe plums
From raspberries, the syrup to sweeten soda,
From gooseberries, the compote, sponge cake, jam,
I suppose you could call Transnistria their coda,

Certainly no more letters ever came
And there was no more anything to long for;
Longing was, itself, a strange taboo
But you couldn't quite help yourself, could you?
All you wanted was one untroubled hour
In the cinema, perhaps, or in a dream

Or wandering, aimless, down adopted boulevards
Oblivious to storefronts, noises, faces,
Trying to piece together shards of words
Scattered over Europe like the scattered beads
Of a thousand trunks of undelivered necklaces,
Bent on mapping out where nowhere leads.

Wherever it is, the way is rich in colors,
Loosely strung with dark pink coral beads,
Littered with fur-trimmed muffs and matching collars,
Crumbs from airy cakes, gooseberry seeds,
Ink stains from a schoolboy's dreaming pen
And pale confetti floating on the Seine

And here is Abe, as he interrupts his wife
Who's describing making brandy out of plums;
To no one in particular he's quoting psalms,
Mumbling about the holiness of life.
What could have happened? He is bruised, distraught,
What could have made him do a thing like that?

On a City I Meant to Visit, Now at War

I heard tales of it on trains, from tireless travelers
And then its name would beckon from the drowsing hulls
Of steamers docked on Venice's back piers
Untroubled by the wild din of gulls.

I could so easily have boarded one
And seen what might have been the stuff of fables,
The spoutings of a circle of medieval whales
Turned, by shipwrecked sorcerers, to stone.

Then I'd have landed on a strange, bright shore
To climb a looming cliff side toward a tower
Whose ramparts seemed to touch the clouds' loose hem
And stare from the turret's jagged diadem

Through exes meant for crossbows in the solid walls
At fishing boats? swimmers? other steamers?
Or rumored clouds of islands linked by still canals
Whose waters dull the wistful coins of dreamers.

I might have watched, from the far side, as the old-town square
Dispatched its slow procession toward a valley
And have seen some of these people, at least in miniature,
Whom we are giving up on almost daily

Or passed them near the marketplace's static clock,
Wiping idle kiosk counters clean
Or looking past the fortress at the trail of smoke
That says they've missed the steamer yet again

Or maybe I'd have gotten on a city bus,
Unfolded my impenetrable map,
And pointed to the museum looking helpless
When a fellow rider would have gotten up,

Gently led me off, taking my wrist,
To herd me on and off a string of trolley cars
And even come along to see the pictures
Like the man who did this once in Budapest

And kissed me on the mouth for quite some time.
Perhaps some years ago he left a bus
With a tourist from the now war-ravaged place
And rode beside her all her long way home

Where, stunned, he hardly knows which side he's on
And cannot lay his hands on any gun.
I wonder why I need his hazy face,
When I can hear, as well as anyone, this teacher's voice,

Saying, on the radio, that she'll starve to death
If she isn't first flattened by a bomb,
That is, until my kettle's mounting steam
Interrupts her with a sudden surge of breath.

Is it heartlessness or just modern science
That enables me to make a cup of tea
While she, just as calm, foretells her death to me?
She deserves, at the very least, perfect silence.

But there's always some noise—a wind, a car,
A household's share of reassuring hums;
I can't invoke pure silence any more
Than I can picture cliffs and palaces and falling bombs,

Which is, let's be honest, what's required here
And I can't even see the cliffs and palaces,
Only jumbled hillsides, roofs and cornices
Borrowed from the cities that I've seen before

And the steamers bobbing near the Grand Canal,
The Hungarian leaving me a last kiss on the cheek,
And in answer to my question *the most beautiful?*
A woman on a train saying *Dubrovnik*

Beijing Rids Itself of Sparrows

An entire city on its rooftops, clanging pans.
The local air has rarely known such clattering:
Pot lids, kettles, caldrons, metal spoons.
It is 1958. Evening. Beijing.

Some can see a bend of river, some a palace;
Some don't look beyond their roofs' red tile;
Some just see a dingy courtyard outhouse;
Others see a rising curve of Wall

As they try to overwhelm the city's sparrows
Who, apparently, won't land where metal clangs,
But fly out frantically from noise to noise
Then hover in the air and beat their wings.

Soon they will expire from exhaustion
Except for those who'll die of broken hearts.
They'll go first; they'll flutter down in unison;
The thick-skinned ones will follow in fits and starts

And Beijing's cats will not believe their eyes,
Their feasts of tiny wings, their one good year,
But the men and women are beyond surprise;
They'll calm their pots and pans and disappear.

Later, of course, they'll mourn in clouds of insects,
Their clanging pots still ringing in their ears
Though there are those—even now, no one suspects—
Who'll long for what they heard as clanging stars

From their vantage on a crashing red-roof ocean,
Themselves a piece of clanging, hooting throng,
A clash of iron for one loved, missing cousin,
A crash for an old nurse's banished song,

A crash for each felled orchard's choicest tree,
A crash for what the coming hour will bring,
Above their heads an undulating, closing sky,
Every inch of it consumed in wing.

Song for the Music
in the Warsaw Ghetto

Pity the tune bereft of singers
Pity the tone bereft of chords
Where shall we weep? By which waters?
Pity the song bereft of words

Pity the harps hung on rifles
The unsuspected cunning in each hand
Pity the shrill, bewildered nightingales
How could they sing in that strange land?

Pity the string that has no bow
Pity the flute that has no breath
Pity the rifle's muted solo
Pity its soundless aftermath

III

London, Before and After: the Middle Way

Where shall I begin, the Metropolitan Line
Or on the South Bank, aimless, all those years ago?
So many cities in my poems, but never London

Though I spent years spying on it from a window
At the top front of a smoky two-tiered bus
In traffic so torturously slow

I'd exchange the daylight for the swifter darkness.
But first, my cortege of houses scaled its hill,
Ladies-in-waiting to the dowager St. Pancras,

Where I'd picture a Victorian giant's doll,
From amidst a life both dutiful and sumptuous,
Peering out a turret at our perfect standstill.

Some days, I'd just linger on the bus,
Vaguely on the watch for random poetry,
Biding my time, postponing hopelessness—

In love with a Londoner who didn't love me—
I'd stay on for the view from Blackfriars Bridge,
The one part of the route the bus took swiftly,

The towers of Parliament a fleet mirage
Of majesty in that expanse of gray,
Squat, terraced houses in their dotage.

London had used up its store of poetry
And etched it on bronze plaques, paved in the ground.
I found them as I drifted down a walkway,

Aimless, on the South Bank, in the wind,
Unnerved every time Big Ben's dull gong
Bellowed out a quarter-hour's end.

Sweete Themmes, runne softly, till I end my Song.
Even then, I knew I'd never write like that—
But I was young; I could imagine I was wrong,

Pleased to have at least a bronze plaque intimate
That I might sing away my wasted yearning.
Real life might not matter to a poet,

Even one whose eyes and face were burning
From the usual clash between events and dreams.
This time, it was children I was mourning—

Imagined so precisely, given names—
All I could do for them was leave them there,
To listen, with the softly running Thames

For whatever it was that had absolved the air,
Momentarily, at least, of gong and wind,
With rumors of a near, persistent *elsewhere* . . .

I was starved for mythic propaganda,
And almost checked for leaflets from that same dim source
In the scraps of paper scattered by the wind.

I'd have gathered them and stuffed them in my purse,
But was cheated, by the quarter-hour gong,
Of my single chance to join the outer universe

And overhear the planets, as they raced along,
Harmonize their pathways' perfect numbers.
I believed in them; I'd seen their music sung.

Perhaps, at the National Gallery, a guard remembers
The girl who used to go to drown her sorrows
Through the longest of those long Italian chambers

To watch those singing angels of Piero's;
They're also in on secrets of geometry;
I later saw the diagrams, the arrows:

The mathematician as painter. He did write theory
But Vasari tells us it was stolen away.
What kind of thief would leave him that Nativity?

Even Europe's schoolchildren on holiday,
Cramming the Gallery on their Easter Tours—
Whom I heard shout, *"il neige," "neve," "Schnee,"*

As a freak snow purified Trafalgar Square's
Slightly dingy bric-a-brac of monuments—
Hushed to see the music of the spheres

Quiver on the angels' startled instruments
And singe each mouth's dark circle with a voice,
While, all around them, geometric arguments

Were resolving themselves into what Pythagoras,
Himself, clearly, a poet of the first rank,
Extracted from the same unyielding muse.

I was listening for it on the riverbank,
Urging grace to be a solid thing,
Afraid I'd blow away, the single blank

Among the crumpled bits and scraps the wind was shuffling.
I used that snatch of poem as a paperweight,
As if some hidden substance made it sing,

Some pure arrangement I could formulate
Like Pythagoras's sleight of hand with triangles—
You square the sides, add them, then take that square root

And you can circumvent unsubtle angles.
I dreamt a kind of lyrical hypotenuse,
Some music I could sing Piero's angels

That might recall a modest phase of Venus
Humming to itself among the stars . . .
My hold on how things worked had grown so tenuous

I was hoping that a lovers' triangle, like ours,
Could also be worked out by an equation.
Or whatever you'd call us. We were no more lovers

Than there were planets in that cluttered din
Of Big Ben, my morning's quarrel, and poetry.
Things aren't what they seem. Or weren't then.

Now, I'm in the middle of the way
Only if my life is fairly long.
I've done my best to remember accurately;

The difficulty, of course, is that the young
Never think of things as irrecoverable.
Bear with me, will you, let me sing one song

Even if it is more suited to a novel:
I have gray hairs, I'm on the Metropolitan Line,
The rooftops of North London at eye level,

It's years since I've been on a train alone,
Letting my mind unravel from a window seat . . .
This morning, I had my children on this same train,

One reading, one asleep beneath her rain hat,
As if there were no panting, giant city.
Picture a doting mother, disheveled, fat,

At best, almost a decent model for Charity:
A dreaming child sprawled across each lap—
Who would even suspect this person of poetry,

Of smiling to herself as she approached the stop
A literary icon had lived near?
But when she's made it up the final step

Trafalgar Square's the same Trafalgar Square.
Perhaps she's just been traveling incognito;
Actually, the Gallery's filled another corner—

A new wing, with a room just for Piero.
Her baby likes the angel Michael's snake;
Her eldest sees *her* in the Leonardo

And for a second she is dazzling, beatific,
Though she knows the child just means her curly hair;
Later, on her own beside the glinting track,

No diaper bag, no favorite toy, no stroller,
Heading to meet her still dear London friends
At a wedding reception in a West End square,

She takes partly as omens, partly, reprimands,
The blurring high-speed trains that hurtle by.
How had she thought that life has open ends?

It is a beauteous evening, calm and free—
But she would never have known this on her own;
She wishes she held stories in her glittering eye

Or, rather, I wish it; by now I'm on the train
And all I'm seeing in the potent glass,
Besides some random lights, is my reflection;

As for the girl who daydreamed on the bus,
Surely she's better off without the tears?
A poet's real life might be superfluous,

But then, it might stretch on and on for years.
How would she have managed? She knew nothing.
I had to trade away her faded spheres

For the earth that had my children on it, breathing.
Even she wouldn't have quarreled with what I did;
In fact—I know her—she'd have traded anything

Which—surely, that's what's happened here—she did
Unless, as in my mind, she hasn't moved
And the earth isn't, in fact, so very solid.

Could things possibly be as she believed?
Suppose I look for her beside the river;
What do I tell her if she has survived,

Has been riding with my children, undercover,
Is here, now, riding on this train,
Having left behind the triangle, the lover,

Grown up, gotten married, had a couple of children
Whom she dragged to see some remnants from her dreams
On the tube from the northern suburbs into London

Where, trying to find a walkway by the Thames,
She listened for a huckster hawking quarter-hours
From a tower with a moonfaced clock and chimes?

I might mention this freak hot spring, its crazed flowers
Blossoming all at once: lilacs with snowdrops,
Crocuses, roses, lilies, jonquils, sunflowers,

Houses with petals jumbled on their stoops
Dreaming dreams they haven't dreamed in years:
Dahlias being asked to dance by tulips

To echoes from the not-so-distant spheres
That, tired of their rarefied isolation,
Have yearned for airplay here on earth for years,

Tried everything: a blizzard, out of season—
The pattern in each slow-dissolving snowflake
An ancient form of musical notation:

The proverbial six sides, no two alike—
Leafleting turrets, bridges, rooftops, domes,
Toppling the starry clusters of a lilac

With variations on a thousand thousand themes.
Think of the music calling from the trees,
The angels calling back from their museums;

Whoever you are, don't stop whatever this is . . .
But what would she have told the spellbound Thames?

Calm Day at Couminole

Wherever it is the ocean's been, from here
It looks as though it's carried off the moon's
Ancestral silver or a low-hung star
Or some neat angel's store of household linens.
And this is not a sea that's known for being calm.
Here, apparently, anything can happen;
I heard a judge describe a meeting with a leprechaun.
Why not a *merrow* in this strange, still foam
That might be a fine tablecloth's fringed edge . . .
Tomorrow, more than likely, it will turn savage
Once again, this ocean, but it *does* now seem
Like a storehouse for the heavens' extra things
Or a host of sleepers having one vast dream,
The bedclothes smooth beneath their folded wings.

On My Third Daughter's
First Night Home

You don't hear it, do you? This urgency?
(The birds are tuning up; it's nearly day.)
For you, it's one more thing to put away
To make sense of in the long, capacious future.
It turns to habit—saving things to come clear
Later—until actually making sense
Of anything becomes a state so rare
You'll attribute it to something out of nature

Like this middle-of-the-night tryst of ours
And what I think I know: the universe
In all its messiness, an open code
Cracked by your particular configuration
Of the usual perfect measure of bone and skin,
Living's wildest promises again made good
And this other thing—which makes me keep you here,
Even though you're sleeping, on this shoulder,

When any sensible person would return to bed—
This knowing that your indistinguishable weight
Will transform itself so fast I won't remember it
Even by the time I write it down;
That's what these raucous birds are on about,
That this blurred precinct—not inside, not out—
Is likely not to last beyond this dawn,
When we'll be, I've known it before, so utterly divided

That we'll forget even what we thought we knew.
Or what I knew rather; knowledge has little to do
With your part, though you seem to have some glimmer
Of more than anyone would give you credit for;
Perhaps you even know that there are far more
Melodious birds than these; there was one
That sounded like some spirit's visitation
On the woods we were living in last summer.

You couldn't hear it; you were far too small;
The air would jangle with a high, brash scale
And before I'd quite discern it, it was gone.
Part of me mistook it for the Greek god Pan
(You'll find I'm given to that sort of thing)
Long before I thought of any bird—
"A thrush," said the locals when I tried to sing
A paraphrase of what I thought I'd heard . . .

Imagine. You could recognize each voice
In the uninflected din I hear as "woods."
I suppose I've been noticing the wrong things.
What was the point of looking out for gods
When a person might untangle any blur of noise
Into who knows how many thousand sets of wings?
I'm hard-pressed to catch even the slimmest hints
When the world lets slip its secret eloquence.

I only heard the thrush because it sounded familiar
Though I didn't place it until afterward—
On a piccolo? ocarina? something high.
The thrush's five-note scale was pure Mozart:
Papageno's birdcall in *The Magic Flute*
No wonder, in the woods, it seemed bizarre.
I like to think that Mozart didn't borrow it
That he and the thrush just did things the same way

But who is to say? Could Mozart hear a bird
With that racket going on inside his head?
I wonder if *he* could write down what he heard,
Or if his final versions were, to him, as crude
As these approximations are to me . . .
Then what would explain my belly turning cartwheels
With your older sister kicking up her heels
In her? my? eighth month, at *Don Giovanni*?

Can the not quite born hear what isn't pure?
I would think impurities come only after,
But then so dauntlessly we're left unsure
Precisely what this *pure* we yearn for is.
Which explains, I suppose, why I'm staying up tonight
Unwilling to turn my back on whatever this is,
A little like some unsuspecting drifter
Who happens upon, say, Petra in the moonlight,

Or a stark red canyon, or the Taj Mahal—
A place he can make no sense of at all,
But is nonetheless disinclined to leave,
Like life itself, I guess, when you come right down
To it, and which is part of this illusion,
That you'll hold on to it for me, I'll achieve
That elusive purity as a shimmery,
If inaccurate, presence in your memory

In eighty years or so when your granddaughter
Clamors for a story about her namesake
And you absolve me of what I'm really like.
Maybe she'll take that gracious portrait with her
Into an as yet uncharted wilderness
About which the only thing I dare to guess
Is that she'll tell a daughter about you
And will also wonder how her life flew

By so fast. Wasn't she the daughter?
Wasn't she the person with the future?
Where had she acquired this mass of anecdotes,
Forsaken projects, overdue accounts?
I hope she's willing to settle for gilded monuments
Since I suspect I'm not among those poets
Who can coax staying power from their rhyme;
As I started to say, I'm running out of time,

And can barely describe you, much less that girl.
For all I know, she'll live on one of those planets
People wanted to call Larry, Moe and Curly;
There'll be no thrush, but she can hear *The Magic Flute*
And read, as he predicted, Shakespeare's sonnets
At some point or other on her circuitous route
To a middle of a night not unlike this
When she'll accept her fleeting bit of grace

And not lament, before it's passed, its passing.
You are, after all, only a frail day old . . .
And have already managed to infuse what I've been told
With truth—albeit tarnished by cliché.
All those lines my wistful mother would say,
As if looking for something, about the years' racing
Now feel, on my lips, like Isaiah's coal—
Which would make you the purifying angel—

Though its intensity is only keen to me,
And no one seeing you sees quite what I see.
Why make all this effort at translation?
When I could bask here in my private vision
And let these birds do my singing for me
Or Ben Jonson: "his best piece of poetry."
How he must have wished he'd never written that
And kept his little seven-year-old with him.

Suddenly I don't want to write a poem.
Much better to change tactics, turn to prayer
For you and your sisters to have what eludes poetry:
A long, safe passage through this dense conspiracy
Of unpredictable, marauding danger.
Probably, love's purest form is terror;
The other kind didn't even last the night.
You see? It's gone. Already you're a stranger

And I can't help you just by breathing air;
Now, I'll have to worry all the time;
I am, as you'll discover, quite a blusterer,
Sending that girl off to an unnamed planet
When I can't even put you in a separate room.
Still, we needn't rock here anymore.
You'll be peaceful in your bassinet.
But your sisters are waking. Listen. That's their door.

Villanelle for the
Middle of the Night

Call it the refrigerator's hum at night,
The even breathing of a sleeping house
As a halo drifts in from a corner streetlight.

Awake, you train an ear to single out
A music jangling just beneath the noise.
Call it the refrigerator's hum at night

Since you have no real hope of being accurate,
But what you mean is usually as diffuse
As a halo drifting from a corner streetlight.

Tonight, though, it is concentrated, intimate,
Luring you to store up what it says
(Call it the refrigerator's hum at night;

That, at least, accommodates the feel of it)
To try to temper yearning into praise,
As a halo drifting from a corner streetlight

Tempts an unsuspecting city street
With its otherworldly armory of shadows.
Call it the refrigerator hums at night,
Call it back. It's drifting mourns the streetlight.

Early Spring, Back in London

The towers of Parliament have new gold skin—
I can't decide if they look lovely or ridiculous.
I remember them a dreary, grayish brown,

As I remember, to tell the truth, the whole metropolis—
And now, everywhere I turn, there's beaten gold—
Bricks, sun, daffodils—as if some frivolous

Saint had pulled her halo from her head and spilled
Its glittering contents slapdash over London.
For once in my life, I'm glad the traffic's stalled

So I can take this random luster in . . .
Though it does hold me up in reaching you,
A dozen bottlenecks away in Stoke Newington

And the reason I took my one-year-old and flew
Across most of a continent and then an ocean . . .
How can I let your far-off saga continue

Without at least my cameo participation
After all we've put each other through?
And then there's your boy—a deviation

From the path you professed and swore you'd stick to
When we'd argue on your dowdy green settee;
I always gave in—it meant much more to you—

The politics, the principles, consistency—
I just meant to keep you there all day
And you didn't really want that much of me

Or did you? In the end, it's hard to say
What either of us was actually after then,
Though it seems like some of it has come our way,

For here we are—the sofa's patterned vine
Peeking out beneath an Indian print
Unable to suppress its sprawl of green—

Clearly we are nothing if not content,
Thrilled, of course, to see each other again.
We have at least done some of what we meant

Though nothing has gone quite according to plan.
We do write, but we don't excite much interest.
And then, of course, there are these children

Just look at them. And look at us—obsessed—
You even more than I, since I have older ones
And one's always most obsessive with the first;

I can be distracted by those ugly grapevines
On your grandmother's? great-aunt's? matched settee and chairs—
The cast-off dishes, cutlery, pots and pans

From a ragtag bunch of attic-cleaning benefactors.
No one but you would use them even then.
To think you haven't replaced them in all these years

Or this flat (a palace to me when
You moved from the squat you'd held illegally
And I lived nowhere, a brief Bohemian

Before my crash landing in the bourgeoisie
Or perhaps I should say my crash return?)
How its cozy imperfections shame me

When I think of my house, my sofa, each lush pattern
On my prized hand-painted Italian crockery . . .
Not that you'd begrudge me my splendid soup tureen

Or any of the other things . . . but what's become of me?
And how did I amass all those possessions
Without once thinking of myself as greedy?

You object when I start making these confessions—
There's your TV, computer, washing machine—
And return to our more heady conversations

About poems, novels, the Party's swift decline.
We don't argue at all. I guess we've mellowed?
Or perhaps we've even learned something since then—

That we needn't utter every thought aloud—
That love can flourish without perfect agreement?
And that this *is* love—how did it manage to elude

Us all those years ago?—is evident
Though it causes no confusion, no desire.
Perhaps it required that we be content,

Having found its wilder incarnation elsewhere,
That we need, finally, nothing from each other
But the kindness of the intervening air.

Though I was right; you were born to be a father.
With your boy you're at your best: dear, hilarious,
Intoxicated even with the endless bother

Of a hundred thousand whimsies as imperious
As the laws of the governments you meant to topple.
For once in my life, I've been victorious

In an argument with you, though I'm not as supple.
The air itself resounds with *I told you so*
As you rush to peel your little boy an apple,

Play the Beatles song he likes, double-knot his shoe . . .
Picking fathers is something I have a genius for
The one I left at home is a virtuoso,

Not that I had a clue what was in store,
That a person could even be as ecstatic
As—with our pack of daughters—we are,

Or that a life that seems wildly frenetic
Can hide a steady underside of calm
(Not to mention his remodeling our attic

Where I will try to put this in a poem
While looking out at mountains topped with snow).
It's not as if I wasn't crazy about him

To begin with. Only there are things you just can't know.
Except I did know. That's why I married him,
Why I'd have married you all those years ago

And here we are—in this same damned room
Where you used to rail against the nuclear family
As the cause of every evil and I would scream

That it was nonsense trumped up for evading me.
And I'm still not sure if I was right or wrong.
How could there have been that much intensity

If you weren't at least tempted to go along
With the stories I'd invent about our children?
How they'd be funny, precocious, clever, headstrong

And so they are: look at them, our children—
And the air (I keep relying on the air,
But it's grown very vocal around our children)

Says that we could have done this thing together—
And also have been happy, done it well
And I'm euphoric, suddenly, rapture everywhere

—lived, unlived—tried, untried—as if all
Life held were so many stores of happiness
That no single person could use them all,

Since neither of us would want to change what is:
That precisely these children should exist
And their siblings, born and unborn (I'm avaricious;

I want many children and I want them blessed).
Besides, we're too far gone—it's our finest trait—
We're loyal people and we love our spouses best

But love is an expansive business, it turns out.
(One does learn something in—what is it? sixteen years?)
Perhaps we simply had to learn the habit.

But how? So often, the habit disappears.
There's a midrash that God, His world now made,
Spends His time putting people into pairs—

I know you hate it when I mention God—
But who knows how an unlived life would be?
Surely, someone sees that this one's good.

Call it love, fatalism, sentimentality.
There is no untried happiness. I was wrong.
How many people are like us, nearing forty

And less bitter than we were when we were young?
Which is not to say we haven't been humbled;
We did expect a good deal of our writing

(I, for one, never planned these wordy, jumbled
Pronouncements swiftly followed by retractions,
But then, let's face it, my thoughts always rambled)

And who could have foreseen the satisfactions
Open even to those who can't express themselves
Or grasp at incompatible abstractions?

Does anyone imagine how the world dissolves
Around a tiny, not quite finished face?
How could we have known that life evolves

In the midst of that absurdly static mess
We make around ourselves when we are young?
Still, I'd have to call that time luxurious:

All that accusation and harangue,
Such fervid, exorbitant expectation.
Our lunatic demands were just the sting

Of a rare, if tortuous, devotion.
At least we managed to escape its being fatal,
If we didn't quite rise to its occasion . . .

Not that I'd ever again, be so brutal —
Though I'm actually fairly vague on what *I* did —
Or ever protect myself so little . . .

I'm clearer on the cruelest thing you said
(Though I know I matched you, cruelty for cruelty).
For me, it's all compressed into one bus ride:

The top deck, front, the seventy-three.
You were going down to your mother's place —
I realize now, to get away from me —

And we rode together as far as King's Cross.
(You remember what you said. I'll leave it out.)
Afterwards, I just stayed on the bus

(You called me to apologize that night;
I was so surprised and touched, I forgave you.
It's the way we are still, isn't it?

No good at staying angry, but compelled to do
These crushing things that we regret so much.
Though not to each other. I think that's through.)

And I remember wondering on that long, gray stretch —
A monotone of streets and bricks and sky —
If the city had arranged itself to match

My spirits from some sort of wayward sympathy
Or whether it was being doubly cruel.
That I was extraneous didn't occur to me;

I'm afraid I was that much of a fool.
And it's tempting now amidst this hoard of gold —
Perhaps I haven't learned much after all —

To wonder if your London hasn't once more pulled
A face — now glorious — entirely for me.
Sandblasters? A different season? Or days now filled

That conspired — years ago — to come up empty?
Or is it that you're finally in this too,
Absorbed in this deliriousness entirely,

Knowing what I wanted you to know,
That these babies running us across Green Park
Displacing every pigeon as they go

Who won't let us browse through a single book
When we finally make our way into a bookstore
Will deliver us—with a reasonable amount of luck—

From that unsatisfactory, elusive elsewhere
That you and I were always hungry for.
Maybe they'll turn out to be that elsewhere.

Maybe—you never know—they always were.
Unless it was this same, now golden, city.
How could we not have known that it was there

Beneath its camouflage of gray-brown, gritty
Residue of factories, buses, cars?
That all those years we fought each other so bitterly

The sky was hysterical with stars
Dressing up as goddesses and speeding bears,
Meddling in all our plans, shaping characters

For God to rearrange into His pairs,
That what is genuine—however muddled—endures,
That even in this climate, weather clears.

Dust on the Mantel: Sonnet

I wonder if the dust collecting here
Remembers breath, how it, too, used to waste
Hours seeming to study the empty air,
Perfecting—or so it thought—the art of daydream
On passersby, weather, cars, stray leaves
As if wholly unsuspecting that a person lives
And dies. How it could talk on the phone,
Watch movies, flip through magazines, this dust.
It even undertook to write a poem
After it settled on a book opened to one
That made a fleeting afternoon stand still.
It braced itself to overhear a voice
Murmur something unequivocally precious.
Who's to say it isn't listening still?

Two Sonnets for the Wind in the Leaves

I.

It comes suddenly, this knowing you've lost your hold
On whatever it was you were certain of
And you can't tell if it's failure to believe
Or just another sign of growing old.
You can't even follow up the hunches
You call memories for lack of better words.
Outside, inconsolable, a linden's branches,
Mysteriously emptied of their birds,
Hear nothing but their own abandoned leaves
Grieving in the wind, asking, bewildered:
Wasn't there music just now? We thought we heard
(It's not even the notes they're after, but proof,
Any explanation for this rush of grief)
A flight of orioles or were they doves?

II.

What I would choose to tamper with, as this wind
Tampers with these trees, is silence, pure silence
If I could find it, and with a deft hand
Leave it just the slightest bit off-balance
So I could at least pretend I heard these rustlings,
The petticoats of muses waiting in the wings
With their dark, unbidden entourage of secrets
Poised to be announced at some lush ball,
Unless they're girls lined up along a wall
In their party dresses, season after season,
With the usual share of misplaced hearts, regrets,
Self-delusions, visions, anxious flurries,
Waiting for anything, a doomed liaison
Or someone, anyone, who'll hear their stories.

Sonnet for a Single Day in Autumn

What was it payment for, the trove of gold
That landed on the lawn outside my door?
And what turned it instantly to oracle:
A heady vision of my study floor
Completely covered over as leaves of gold
Came flying off my printer, singing odes
Obliquely tuned to an improvident God's
Unwillingness to stint His taste for miracle
Despite our constant failure at belief.
This was what the angels use—gold leaf—
To plug the hairline fractures in their halos.
If only they'd gathered some before the snow's
Extravagantly surreptitious siege
Hushed them with its supple empty page.

On a Bus,
Visiting Amherst from Salt Lake City

Perhaps it isn't quite the stuff of sonnets —
The back roads, village by village, on a bus —
But these are the hills that once untied their bonnets.
Not that I can see any sign of this,
But poems are often for what we can't see
And — I guess I'm one of those self-appointed apprentices —
This is yet another poem for Emily.
I thought she'd like to know about the giantesses
That dwarf the little city where I live,
Their heads in thick, wool shawls, her favorite white,
How, yesterday, in my view from up above
They looked like one enormous crumpled sheet.
For all I know it's Emily's new bed,
Glaciers at her feet, clouds at her head.

Calling Emily Dickinson to Come, as Guide, Out West

Certainly, you're a strange choice for a guide,
A painfully timid woman who's been nowhere,
Rarely, for years at least, even outside.

But there are things I want to know about the air
And by all accounts you and she were intimate;
She'd slip in late at night to braid your hair

And with every twisted strand divulge a secret.
Perhaps it was her rendezvous with thunder
That urged you into your one wild night.

Who knows how far afield she helped you wander?
Perhaps she introduced the sea, the moor,
The way the heather's reckless bells meander

To the brinks of cliffs to ring the waves ashore.
Perhaps she even learned to mimic their chime
Or brought a tiny perfumed souvenir

Right through the opened window to your room.
After that you never wanted to leave.
I should like a grand tour of that room:

The tricks of swallows orbiting the eave,
The most elaborate ceiling cracks and floorboards,
The piles and piles of poems you didn't save

But distributed, instead, among the birds
Who promised to pass them on to flies and bees.
In those, perhaps, you didn't stoop to words.

They were pure reverie, like your prairies.
You'd show those, too, if the tour were thorough
And pens cut from the feathers of passing geese,

Each an instantaneous perfect arrow
That would overwhelm its mark at breakneck speed
And, without harming a bone, pluck its marrow.

You needn't be a specter in the Underworld.
(You don't believe in it, do you? Nor do I.)
But I'm hoping you'll be willing to make a trade:

If you'll just show me how to shoot one bull's-eye
And introduce that friend of yours, the air,
I'll bring you to an open tract of sky

And wildness you can't have dreamed was here
In this, your own, our own, unlikely country.
Surely reports came through that you would hear,

Lavinia would read them out loud in the pantry
While you were making puddings or baking bread,
The view outside the window placid, wintry;

You'd look dreamy-eyed but shake your head.
Such preposterous tales of breadth and width and height.
But they were true. I'll show you. *I'll* be guide —

We'll reverse Dante and Virgil — while *you* write.
You see, I'm not quite up to what I've seen.
I should have stayed at home, always worn white,

But there was so much out there, Emily, and I like green.
Besides, I want to know what you'd have made —
If a garden snake is *Zero at the Bone* —

Of hordes of spires of rock, all scalded red,
The wicked turned by spirits into stone
Or so the local people have always said.

If only they'd turned all Amherst into stone
And the tone-deaf editors who changed your rhymes.
You wouldn't have had to stay up there alone

And might have known how landscape climbs and climbs
Until you have no vantage point, no explanation
Except what you can summon from the Psalms.

And the land in maps that press their way to ocean
Turns out to be covered in endless sage
That goes silver at the slightest provocation.

How will you travel over it? By train? By stage?
Perhaps you'll choose a huge hot-air balloon?
How will you fit the dashes on the page

That describes your first liaison with a canyon?
Don't look so bewildered. I've read your poem.
I know you claim that these things needn't be seen.

But this absurd superfluity of room
Is precisely what it means to be American
And not a square inch in it for a poem.

That's why I need you for a chaperon.
For me, you see, before I came out West
You were what it meant to be American

And I didn't know if I was cursed or blessed —
To sit up in a garret on your own,
All that stunning marksmanship unnoticed.

But I had you. You'd written what you'd written.
I wanted to live in that same country.
I liked to think that we had things in common

And it didn't seem so long to wait—a century—
To have one's book on every library's shelf.
In my own way, I'm just as greedy as Dante,

Trying to have you here all to myself.
Dante at least was worthy of his guest
While I am stuck with this colossal gulf—

Not just this vast expanse from West to East
But my wordiness, my clumsiness, my *life*.
Virgil came to Dante as a ghost

But I wanted to bring you here *alive*
And you such a shy woman and I so brazen,
With nothing to give you. I don't even drive,

Barely know the West. I'm its newest citizen.
Besides, you're right. A poet needn't see.
If I actually thought I'd made you listen

I'd have to beg you wildly to forgive me
For barging in like this with such poor aim,
Dreaming I could imitate your bull's-eye,

Going without permission to your room
(It's true, Emily, I've already been there)
And publishing books of poems in my lifetime

Without even having met your friend the air,
Not to mention daring to write down your name
And pretending, for an instant, you might hear.

Summer Night: Flamenco

The crickets sound like distant castanets
And I imagine heels crashing in some far
High grass and foaming skirts, a swarm of hornets
Panicking inside a locked guitar.
Even the local stars are in a panic,
Clapping out a *paso doble* for dear life,
Percussion for the moon's earsplitting cry.
It could be that the heat's hallucinogenic,
But I actually think it's pure flamenco.
Just listen as its off-rhythm staccato
Pulses through our bodies with the strict, slow riff
Of the air's tight spiral between us and sky,
Its inward-outward circuit of desire
Singed by near, quick-spreading wildfire.

Breezeway, circa 1964

The leisurely fireworks of fireflies,
The cicadas rattling the trees,
The crickets' slow, relentless high-note, low-note,
All this from a stoop in Philadelphia
In a heat so encompassing, so endless,
The mauve between the power lines is motionless
Though dusk is several evenings overdue.
Still, no mother calls us from a window;
Not even a radio cries out.

Nothing. No minute is allowed to pass.
So how is it that I'm no longer there,
Mistaking the cicadas for a shift of power
Surging through an overhanging wire,
The crickets for some mild, more muffled traffic?
Such lazy stars have settled in our lawn,
On again, off again, until a strange dark moon
Entices them to join the spreading darkness . . .
It's an ordinary evening—nothing mythic,

Not even a memorable neighborhood. Each house
Repeats its homely, semidetached face
As if the matching street front were a mirror.
I only ever wanted to get out of there.
So what, exactly, am I longing for?
Fireflies? Cicadas? Sultry air?
(I still don't understand. Can it be over?)
The sleek rococo of a passing car.
Another summer night that lasts forever.

V

Sonnet about
Last Night's Moon beneath the Clouds

Take the moon last night beneath the clouds,
How it made them seem like alabaster hoods
On some eminence trying to make a getaway—
In this case, striking out for open sky
Which doesn't really use its light so well.
Even though it was a day short of full
It was still enough to leave me reassured
That I'm not entirely wasting my one life.
Pure luck, I suppose, that it was unobscured
By any of the neighboring trees and that my roof
Was gracious enough, this year, to admit a skylight
Which itself was gracious enough to admit a moon
That turned whatever it entered to a field of white
Where—who knows?—something holy might have been.

Full Moon over Salt Lake City:
Seven-thirty A.M.

What are you doing here, my dear, my sweet
All decked out in canary yellow?
I can't wear that color; my skin's too sallow
But maybe you'd let me borrow that shimmery white
Gauzy number you were out in late last night.
I must say, this yellow suits you; you're aglow.
And the puny little skyline just below
You makes you huge. That white thing wouldn't fit.
It wouldn't, now that I think of it, fit me either.
Besides, it's a bit too skimpy for this weather;
Do you feel that chill? It's really fall.
But it's seven-thirty in the morning; where's the sun?
You got her plastered—didn't you?—at the Harvest Ball.
Quick. You'd better give her back her gown.

Sonnet to the New Moon

According to the calendar, you're out of town
(This morning was the prayer for the New Moon)
So what can explain the windows' milky glow—
At—what is this?—two o'clock in the morning?
Oh, I see: it's tomorrow's promised snow;
For once, they were right to give us warning,
Though we weren't meant to heed it quite this soon.
Look at our linden tree, it's in a swoon;
It can't tell the difference between earth and sky
And I'll tell you something, moon, neither can I,
Not that I believe you really have no share
In this milkiness, this dreamy borrowed light.
Maybe these are tendrils drifting through the air
From when you trimmed your hair the other night. . . .

Terza Rima for
a Sudden Change in Seasons

Probably God laughs at us, down here, entranced
As, to quiet us, He tosses down another season,
And we ooh and ah—like infants silenced

By the jangling of keys above a playpen—
At the all-effacing green or white or gold,
Or even something small: a stem, a robin,

A brittle smattering of stars across a field,
As if we hadn't seen it all a year ago
And every year before that, since an arm first held

Us to a startling, milky window, saying, "snow."
Maybe it started as a temporary subterfuge,
To distract us while He carved each gaudy *no*

In the tablets he was making for His protégé.
He never dreamed that we'd have been so thick.
Hadn't he made us in His own image?

Could this possibly be what He was like:
Utterly bamboozled, year after year,
By the same, not all that complicated, trick?

Once you tilt the earth's revolving sphere
The rest of the stuff is pretty automatic . . .
But who could have imagined all our fanfare,

The way each unhinged leaf makes us poetic,
Or a single, all-inclusive blast of snow?
Especially here, in my converted attic,

The skylights blank with white, the wall-sized window
Which usually lets in every local circumstance
Just framing what the trees no longer know.

(They've forgotten where their branches are, for instance,
The houses, fences, toolsheds, swing sets, power lines,
The stiff cabal of mountains in the distance.)

What can God be doing with these afternoons,
With us so busy ogling the newest change
That we don't bother Him with choirs, organs, carillons,

Petitions for forgiveness, cash, revenge —
Maybe He's trying to write another book
In which Ishmael and Esau finally avenge

Themselves, Hagar and Leah get another look
And it's revealed that on those forty nights
When Moses was supposedly on Sinai, he really took

Several whirlwind tours of Canaan's highlights —
Hebron, Jericho, Moriah, Zion,
The usual tourist binge of the holy sites

That he was meant to glimpse from atop a mountain;
God didn't have the heart to keep him out.
Unless, perhaps, it took greater compassion

To spare Moses from having to find out
That the Promised Land was just another place.
From a mountaintop, you can remain in doubt

Of a region's basic ordinariness —
What city doesn't look best from a distance?
No stench, no cars, no cockroaches, no mice,

Just towers, bridges, seeming effervescence,
The unobstructed line of each facade . . .
As if Moses were on Bellosguardo, seeing Florence

Or staring at Manhattan from the Promenade;
I know He's supposed to be autonomous,
But maybe this was the only way that God

Could seem to make good on His crazy promise.
That's when He got smart and thought of winter,
Spring, summer, autumn, each one luminous

In its peculiar way, that it might counter
Our inevitable disappointment in the land itself
As our Egyptian memories grew fainter . . .

Or maybe it was a way of distancing Himself.
To keep us in awe or for self-protection?
Perhaps He never recovered from the Golden Calf,

Or maybe, like everyone else, He fears rejection,
Perfectly justifiable, when you consider the trend
That began with Lyell and natural selection—

A laborsaving device that got out of hand.
It was only meant to apply to moths and tortoises;
The various human races were supposed to blend,

God assumed that all our obvious likenesses
Would outweigh any differences that might arise,
Our few disputes smoothed over with the courtesies

To which the carved stone tablets would give rise—
Let's say God got in over His head,
Which really shouldn't be much of a surprise

Since He couldn't even be sure a thing was good
Until He'd gone ahead with its creation.
You'll remember He called us very good,

Which suggests His judgment is a bit in question,
Or, perhaps, that He had no alternatives;
He didn't have much stomach for destruction.

Unless that's just another front; maybe He thrives
On floods, earthquakes, genocides, jihads —
Maybe He put us here to make explosives,

Made science just an ornate set of leads
In an ongoing pursuit of perfect ruin.
After all, He promised, no more floods . . .

Maybe He wanted to see if atomic fission
Was any good. Why else create uranium?
Unless it's just a ploy for more attention

(It's been ages since anyone wrote a psalm)
Or another stopgap, like the seasons,
While He works out some unexpected problem:

Who knows? Perhaps He's running out of hexagons —
Has no idea what He will do for snow;
Maybe all these flakes out here have twins,

And He's afraid that, sooner or later, we'll know
That there isn't really any infinite thing.
Clean hands? A pure heart? I don't think so

But maybe if one of us got up to sing
Or even hummed a tune, say Vivaldi,
Or plucked it out on some obliging string —

You know the one, the winter melody,
The tour de force for solo violin —
He'd make this next millennium a bit less bloody,

Find some calmer version of adrenaline.
But maybe we can't blame Him; He's lost His way,
Gotten bogged down in crocus, lily, dandelion,

Unable to keep the spring's demands at bay
While another hemisphere clamors for fall;
The trees, without His help, refuse to sway,

The birch leaves won't go gold, won't thin, won't fall . . .
He's far too overworked to listen to us.
But He must hear something sometimes. A mating call?

Traffic? Rain? A graceful turn of phrase?
I bet He takes a break when there's a nightingale.
Perhaps He'll linger for a song of praise.

Somebody Ought to
Write a Poem for Ptolemy

Somebody ought to write a poem for Ptolemy,
So ingenious in being wrong, he was almost a poet.
Can anyone follow his configurations?
How he cut a tortured path for every planet
Until his numbers matched what he could see,
Every one spectacularly wrong.
You would think, in all those years of calculations,
He would, at least, have suspected a simpler way.
Maybe he even knew it all along—
The stationary sun, ellipses, everything—
But kept it to himself as too unseemly
Or to save his pregnant wife from all that spinning
And wait beside her in a quiet place
That he, himself, had rendered motionless.

Moses in Paradise

And they saw the God of Israel and underneath
His foot it was like a brickwork of sapphire
and the sky itself for purity.

EXODUS 24:10

You'll laugh when I tell you how I spend my time here
(I'm still not used to it; such greens and blues
And no one buzzing orders in my ear)

I read poetry: Ezekiel's, David's, Isaiah's;
I love the burning coals, the threats, the bones
And the way insatiable David offers praise

Not only from himself, but skies and mountains . . .
How can he know for certain what a palm
Tree wants? An island? Bolts of lightning? Stones?

But what could have induced such gloomy wisdom
In David's subtle-minded jaded son?
Surely, he didn't intend to back a claim

Like *there is nothing new under the sun.*
Up here, there's a new poem every week
(Though never as wondrous as *what's with you, ocean*

That you ran away; Jordan, that you fell back?)
I remember an Italian one we made a lot of—
It's a pity I'm too old to learn to speak

But it was enough to hear those smooth vowels move
In and out of cadences, like muffled chimes.
Still, I suspect they dwelt too much on love

Which is not—despite those clever triple rhymes—
Take it from me—really a divine motive.
God doesn't much go in for simple themes

And I don't think He ever bothers to give
Particular thought to how a person feels,
For example, what it might be like to leave

Whatever it is you know: the clump of hills
That goes purple in the half-light, even at Goshen . . .
Not that He wasn't kind to me; His calls

Were never loud or pushy, and He showed compassion
At my sluggishness in getting stories down.
(I was never very good at taking dictation.)

Once, he even let *me* write a line—
It was after the strangest thing I heard him dictate:
And they saw the God of Israel. He then went on

With something else entirely and I blurted out
But surely you won't just leave it hanging there?
Then I looked up *and underneath His foot*

It was like a brickwork of sapphire
And the sky itself for purity . . . and God
Humored me and murmured in my ear

You like that? Write it down. Go ahead.
My eight words in Exodus. My poem.
Every chance I got, I'd scroll back and read

Them out again; I'd even try to chant them;
Nights, I'd find them in the names the stars
Had scrawled across sky's graffitied dome . . .

My dreams were crammed with feet, skies, sapphires,
Each with such a flair for deviation,
If only you could know them all without the scars

Of my slightly bumbling scribe's English translation
(*Etzem*, you see, means *itself, essence, bone*).
I found her working out the cantillation;

She'd stopped at my eight words, overthrown,
So I had to use her, though her Hebrew's imprecise
And you can't say in English: *heaven's bone*

Which is what I meant to get at: the eeriness
Of its solid and unyielding white interior,
What Ezekiel calls *the eye of terrible ice*

Which he sees under *the appearance of a sapphire* —
Coincidence? — *upon the likeness of a throne* —
I'd like to think my poem might have helped inspire

His vision, but I know he saw that throne.
That throne, those rising bones, the wheels in wheels,
The wings of eyes, the creatures — all his own.

Maybe I should have tried eating scrolls
But that was not what God had in mind.
My lot was mine; Ezekiel's was Ezekiel's

And neither one involved a promised land.
For poor Ezekiel it was just bad luck
While I actually bungled a command;

You know the story: I had to tell a rock—
The people were thirsty—to bring forth water.
But all I could think of when I tried to speak

Was: imagine, rock, that you're a sapphire;
Imagine that you close your hard blue eye
And feel God's foot exert its slightest pressure.

How the pure sky within you starts to liquefy
How the earth around you celebrates, soaked through . . .
Those same paltry words: foot, sapphire, sky;

David's boy was right—there's nothing new.
I thought my heart would break from its own aridity—
It belongs in the desert it condemned me to—

And struck the rock for failing to inspire me.
I didn't deserve to enter the Promised Land
Though I wish I could've stayed in the vicinity

Long enough to see a bunch of grapes that spanned
Two poles carried by giants. Even here
There's nothing quite so worthy of a legend.

But I wouldn't have found the words for it either.
If God was grooming me to be a poet,
I'm afraid He was something of a failure.

All I ever really managed was anecdote—
Though not for lack of trying—however vivid.
I don't blame God for growing so remote

And spending all His spare time coaching David.
I have no complaints; I'm heaped with fame.
Anyway—I wrote it—it's forbidden to covet

Other people's things, even a psalm.
Besides, which would I choose? They're all so luminous
And not a single sapphire among them.

Still, I have no good reason to be envious.
Every other Chasid bears my name.
There's even a church named for me in Venice

And David's friend in Florence who did so well by him
Made me a better likeness, even with its horns.
And I've seen splendid things: the still-green stem

That cools the heart of anything that burns,
The sapphire footpath underneath the sea,
The fish retreating, flashy as the gemstones

On my princess's fingers as she'd fondle me.
She always pledged to give me one someday;
I was hoping for the lapis lazuli,

But then I killed a slave driver and ran away—
How could I have done it?—and Pharaoh's son,
Who used to take me swimming every Wednesday . . .

(I remember he would leave his headdress on
So I would catch a glimpse, with every breath,
Of sunlight on its hem of sapphire stone.)

Perhaps he would have grown more like his father—
That was, after all, what he was groomed for—
But I could so easily have stopped his death

With a simple bloody mark on his chamber door
Though it would, needless to say, have spoiled everything;
I did what I was told, no less, no more.

It's hard to break a lifetime's habit of listening
Which is why I subscribe to David's concert series;
He's got something booked for every evening

And he's very open-minded. He once asked the Furies
(A fiasco—the noise was overpowering)
And, when Deborah canceled, Mohammed's houris,

Who were wonderful to watch but couldn't sing;
We even heard my sister's tambourine last night
And afterwards Isaiah sang a lovely thing

About the beauty of the mountains beneath the feet
Of any messenger who brings good news.
Did I tell you? David's asked me for tonight

And, well, really, what have I got to lose?
He promised to accompany me on the lyre.
Do you think there's something here that I might use?

I could teach it in a hour to the choir.
They learn quickly and their diction is sublime.
But I wish I had a bit more of a repertoire;

You never know—do you?—who might come.
I was hoping I might catch a glimpse of sapphire
Beneath a tapping foot, keeping time . . .